AF118644

FROM
TO

Olympia

FROM
TO

POSTAL
STATION
FROM
TO

POSTAL
STATION
FROM

Olympia

POSTAL
STATION
TO
FROM

FROM
TO

FROM
TO

FROM

TO
FROM

POSTAL STATION
FROM

FROM
TO

FROM

Olympia

POSTAL
STATION
FROM
TO

POSTAL STATION
FROM

POSTAL STATION
FROM
TO

FROM

POSTAL STATION
FROM
TO

FROM
TO

POSTAL
STATION
FROM
TO

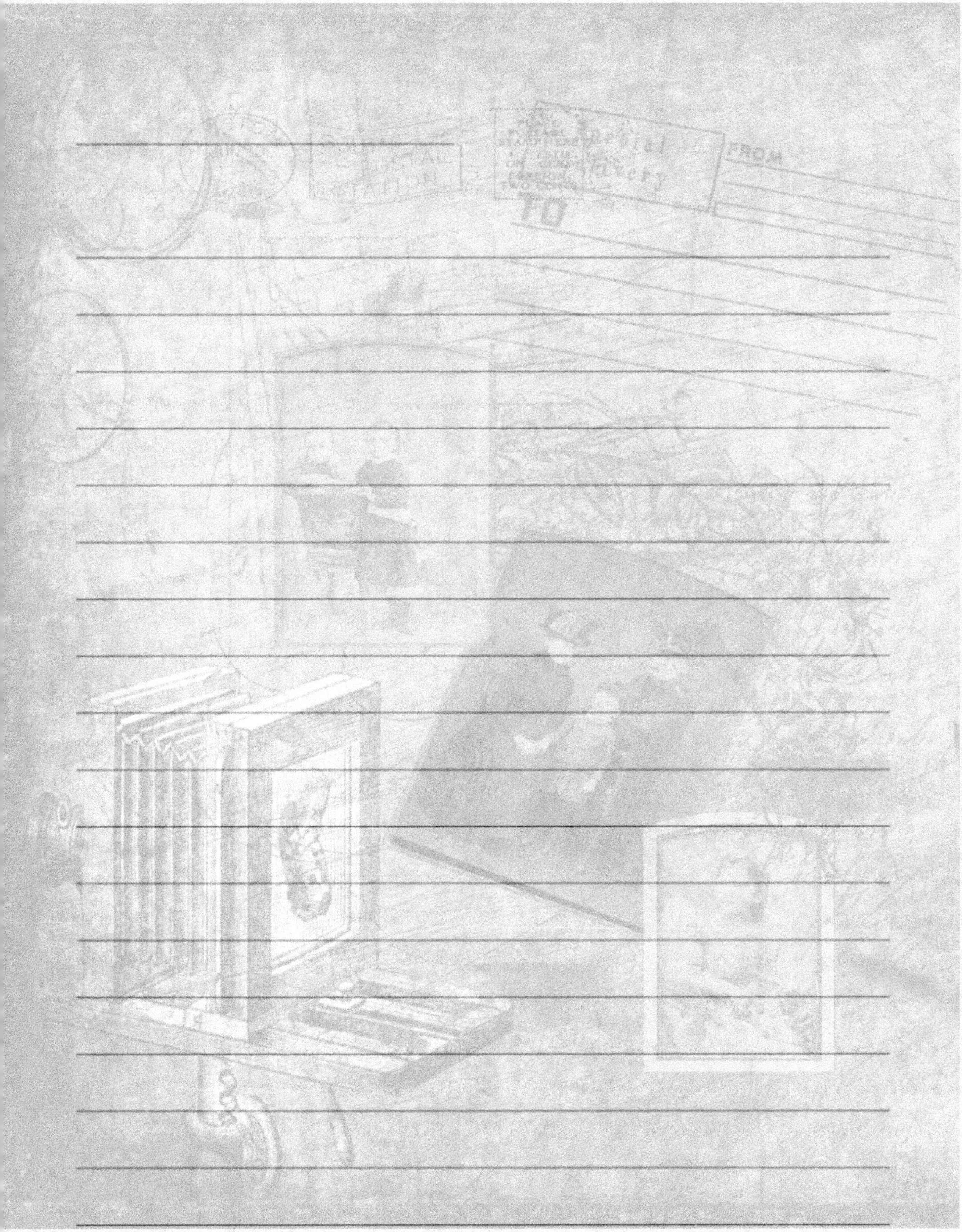
FROM

Olympia

FROM
TO

FROM
TO

FROM
TO

STATION
FROM
TO

FROM
TO

FROM

POSTAL
STATION
FROM

FROM

POSTAL
STATION
FROM
TO

Olympia

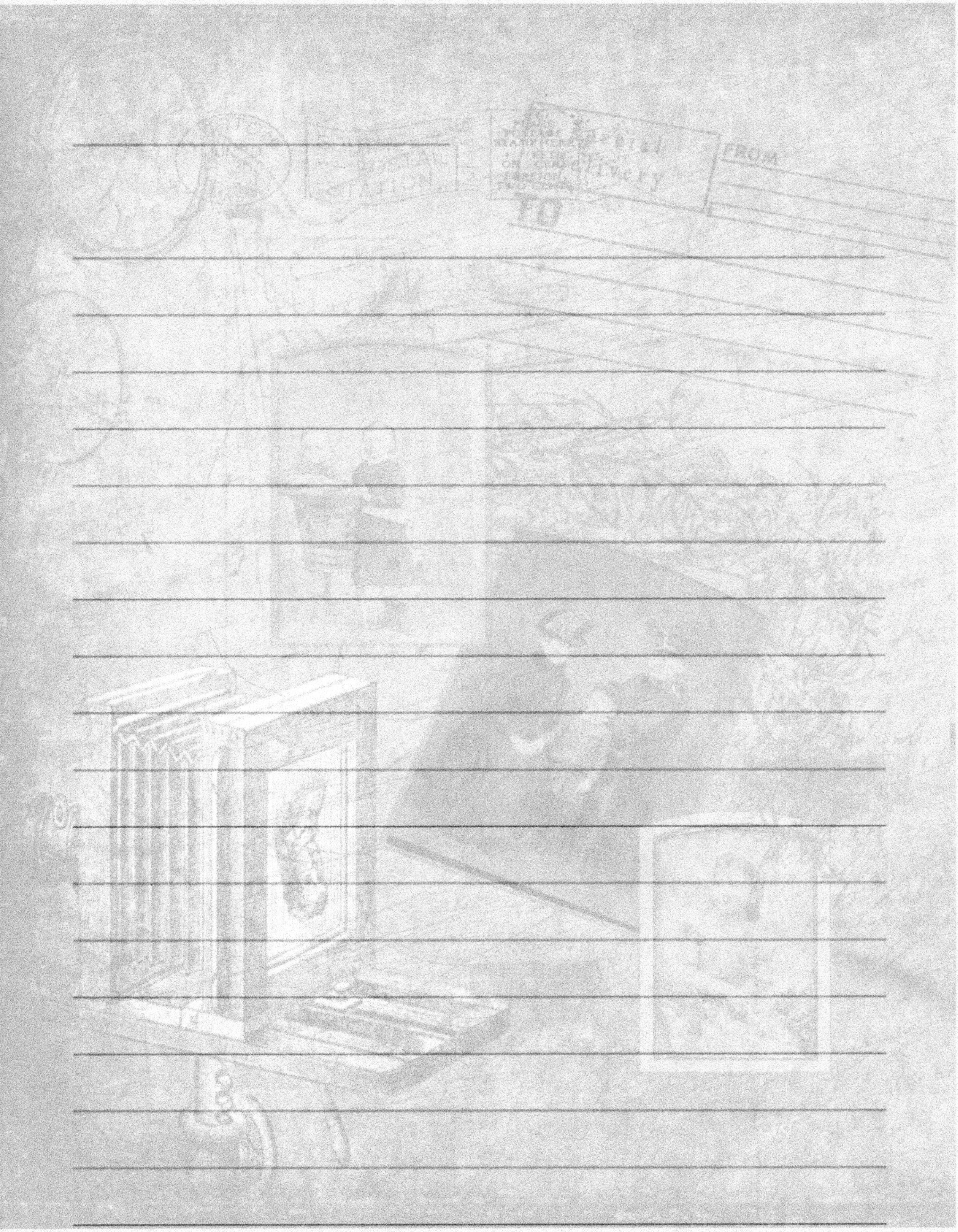
POSTAL STATION
FROM

FROM
TO

Olympia

FROM
TO

POSTAL
STATION
TO
FROM

POSTAL
STATION
FROM
TO

POSTAL STATION
FROM
TO

FROM
TO

FROM
TO

FROM

POSTAL
STATION
FROM
TO

FROM

POSTAL
STATION
FROM
TO

POSTAL
STATION
FROM

POSTAL STATION
TO
FROM

Olympia

POSTAL
STATION
TO
FROM

FROM
TO

Olympia

FROM

FROM
TO

FROM
TO

POSTAL STATION
FROM

FROM
TO

FROM

Olympia

FROM

POSTAL STATION
FROM
TO

Olympia

FROM

POSTAL
STATION
TO
FROM

FROM
TO

FROM
TO

Olympia

FROM

POSTAL
STATION
FROM
TO

FROM
TO

FROM
TO

FROM
TO

POSTAL
STATION
FROM
TO

FROM
TO

FROM
TO

FROM

FROM

POSTAL
STATION
FROM

POSTAL
STATION
TO
FROM

FROM
TO

Olympia

POSTAL
STATION
TO
FROM

Olympia

STATION
TO
FROM

Olympia

FROM
TO

FROM

FROM
TO

Olympia

FROM
TO

POSTAL
STATION
FROM
TO

FROM
TO

POSTAL
STATION
FROM
TO

FROM
TO

FROM
TO

Olympia

FROM
TO

FROM
TO

FROM

FROM
TO

FROM
TO

POSTAL
STATION
FROM
TO

FROM

POSTAL STATION
TO
FROM

POSTAL
STATION
TO
FROM

FROM
TO

FROM
TO

POSTAL
STATION
FROM
TO

FROM

FROM
TO

FROM
TO

Olympia

POSTAL
STATION
FROM
TO

FROM
TO

POSTAL STATION
FROM
TO

www.ingramcontent.com/pod-product-compliance
Lightning Source LLC
LaVergne TN
LVHW060139080526
838202LV00049B/4029